Simple Be Cookbook for Everyone

Gourmet Bento Box Lunchbox Recipes

BY: Allie Allen

COOK & ENJOY

Copyright 2019 Allie Allen

Copyright Notes

This book is written as an informational tool. While the author has taken every precaution to ensure the accuracy of the information provided therein, the reader is warned that they assume all risk when following the content. The author will not be held responsible for any damages that may occur as a result of the readers' actions.

The author does not give permission to reproduce this book in any form, including but not limited to: print, social media posts, electronic copies or photocopies, unless permission is expressly given in writing.

My Gift to You for Buying My Book!

I would like to extend an exclusive offer to receive free and discounted eBooks every day! This special gift is my way of saying thanks. If you fill in the subscription box below you will begin to receive special offers directly to your email.

Not only that! You will also receive notifications letting you know when an offer will expire. You will never miss a chance to get a free book! Who wouldn't want that?

Fill in the subscriber information below and get started today!

https://allie-allen.getresponsepages.com/

Table of Contents

Simple Bento Recipes 7

1) Deep Fried Pork Cutlets 8

2) Teriyaki Chicken with Roasted Mushroom Cap 11

3) Salmon Furikake Sushi Bento 14

4) Chikuwa Cucumber 18

5) Gomashio Cookie 20

6) Cheeseburger Cups 23

7) Shuumai Dumplings 26

8) Lemony Basil Orzo Pasta Salad 29

9) Earl Grey Tea Muffins 31

10) Black Forest Ham and Caramelized Onion Grilled Cheese 34

11) Tamagoyaki 36

12) Sweet Hot Mustard and Jarlsberg Grilled Cheese 38

13) Apple Bunny 40

14) Chicken Taco... 42

15) Sautéed Spinach.. 44

16) Mediterranean Tuna Salad 46

17) Basic Taco Meat Mix 49

18) Vegetable Pickle Salad 52

19) Bacon-Wrapped Asparagus....................................... 54

20) Rafute Rillettes 56

21) Sweet Stewed White Beans....................................... 59

22) Sesame Flavored Beef with Carrot Kinpira 61

23) Walnut Miso Paste for Cooked Vegetables 64

24) Vegetable Frittata.. 66

25) Mini Cabbage Rolls 69

26) Mushroom Rice and Lemon Chicken Nugget Bento 73

27) Mini-Meatloaves... 77

28) Panfried Komachibu.. 80

29) Poppy Seed Encrusted Green Pea Mini-Burgers 82

30) Pan-fried Crispy Chicken Nuggets with Gobo 85

About the Author 88

Author's Afterthoughts 90

Simple Bento Recipes

sssssssssssssssssssssssssssssssssssssssssssss

1) Deep Fried Pork Cutlets

Deep fried pork cutlets are called Tonkatsu in Japanese. This bento lunch box is paired with some stir fried shredded cabbage seasoned with salt and pepper, along with a few store bought pickled peppers topped with goat cheese and mayonnaise.

Makes: 2 cutlets

Cooking Time: 15 minutes

List of Ingredients:

- Pork cutlets, 2, boned
- Panko breadcrumbs, 1 cup
- Egg, 1, beaten
- Salt, to taste
- Flour, for coating
- Pepper, to taste
- Peanut oil, for frying

ssssssssssssssssssssssssssssssssssssssssssssss

Instructions:

Trim any excess fat if needed.

Slice the entire cutlet slightly. Don't make deep cuts.

Season with salt and pepper.

Coat the cutlets in flour then egg and lastly in breadcrumbs.

Deep fry in peanut oil until golden brown and crispy.

Transfer on paper towel to drain excess oil and slice into long pieces while it's still hot.

Pack in the bento when it's cooled down.

2) Teriyaki Chicken with Roasted Mushroom Cap

Teriyaki chicken can be prepared overnight, however roasted mushroom caps needs to be fresh so you have to prepare them in the morning. They will take hardly 10 minutes of your time. Pack mushrooms and chicken with blood orange and rice.

Makes: 1

Cooking Time: 10 minutes

List of Ingredients:

- Chicken cubes, 1 cup
- Soy sauce, 2 tsp.
- Mirin, 2 tsp.
- Sugar, 1 tsp.

For Chevre Mushroom Caps:

- Pancetta, 4 tsp., cubed
- Broccoli rabe leaves, 3 tbsp., chopped
- Garlic, ½ clove, minced
- Butter, 1 tsp.
- Goat cheese, 2 tbsp., softened
- Mushroom caps, 3

ssssssssssssssssssssssssssssssssssssssssssssssss

Instructions:

Grease a pan with oil and cook chicken until brown.

Add soy sauce sugar and mirin. Combine well and cook until meat is tender.

To make mushroom caps, melt butter in a pan and sauté garlic, pancetta and broccoli leaves.

Transfer the contents in a bowl and add cheese. Use a fork to mix everything together.

Stuff mushroom caps with this mixture and place them in a toaster oven broiler until roasted and turn brown.

Pack in the bento box with rice.

3) Salmon Furikake Sushi Bento

Don't worry if you don't own a hangiri or a rice cooker. Sushi rice can easily be cooked in a conventional pot and hangiri can be substituted with a large bowl. Always use a wooden spatula to fold the rice with sushi vinegar to retain its glossy texture.

Makes: 2

Cooking Time: 30 minutes

List of Ingredients:

For Salmon Furikake:

- Raw salmon fillet with skin, 1, 150 g
- Light soy sauce, 2 tsp.
- Sake, ½ cup + 1 heaping tbsp.
- Mirin, 1 tbsp.
- Salt, to taste

For Sushi Rice:

- Japonica rice, 2 cups
- Dashi stock, 2 ¼ cups
- Sushi vinegar, ¼ cup

sssssssssssssssssssssssssssssssssssssssssssssss

Instructions:

Rub salt on each side of the fillet and refrigerator for 60 minutes.

Place fillet in a nonstick pan with skin side facing the bottom.

Add sake and cover with the lid. Steam cook on medium heat.

Transfer the steamed fish on a plate and flake it using a fork, also discard any bones you find.

Clean the pan and place the fish back in it.

Add 1 heaping tbsp. of sake, soy sauce and mirin. And cook until flaky.

To prepare sushi rice, drain and rinse rice at least 3 times or until the water turns clear.

Strain in a mesh sieve and keep aside for 30 minutes.

Now transfer rice in a rice cooker and add dashi stock and allow it to stand for another 15 minutes.

Cook rice on high for a minute then turn the heat to medium and cook for 5 minutes. Lastly, turn the heat low and cook until the water has dried out.

Transfer rice into a hangiri and stir sushi vinegar. Work fast and mix rice with the vinegar. Make sure you do not mush the rice while mixing.

4) Chikuwa Cucumber

Chikuwa are long fish cakes popular in Japan and are part of Japanese cuisine. Stuffing these long fish cakes with cucumber pieces makes a quick and easy side dish for your bento lunch box.

Makes: 5 fish cakes

Cooking Time: 5 minutes

List of Ingredients:

- Japanese/English cucumber, 1
- Chikuwa (Japanese fish cake), 1 package

sssssssssssssssssssssssssssssssssssssssssssssss

Instructions:

Slice the edges of the cucumber to make it the same length as chikuwa and peel off the skin.

Slice the cucumber crosswise into 5 pieces and scoop out the seeds from each piece.

Now put each cucumber piece inside chikuwa and slice it into medium size pieces.

5) Gomashio Cookie

Gomashio is a sesame salt, therefore these cookies are not even close to tasting sweet. They are salty and are good for people avoiding sugar. You can prepare the cookie dough a night before and just bake it the next morning to save time.

Makes: 12 cookies

Cooking Time: 15 minutes

List of Ingredients:

- Butter, 1.75 oz.
- Soymilk, 2-4 tbsp.
- Gomashio, 2 heaping tbsp.
- All-purpose flour, 3.5 oz.

ssssssssssssssssssssssssssssssssssssssssssssss

Instructions:

Preheat the oven to 360 F.

Place a parchment paper on a baking sheet and keep aside

Put butter in a plastic bag and work with your hands to cream it.

Add gomashio and combine well.

Add flour and form a crumbly mixture.

Gradually pour milk and combine well to make smooth dough.

Make a big block of the dough by evenly straightening the edges.

Refrigerate for 30 minutes.

Remove plastic and cut the dough into 12 pieces and assemble on the prepared baking sheet.

Bake for 15 minutes or until the cookies turn brown and becomes firm.

6) Cheeseburger Cups

These mini cheeseburgers will fit perfectly in a bento lunch box. This recipe is simple and can be made in the morning if you have enough time. Just prepare the dough and beef overnight and do the baking next morning.

Makes: 6 burgers

Cooking Time: 20 minutes

List of Ingredients:

For Burger Mix:

- Ground beef, 1 pound
- Brown sugar, 2 tbsp.
- Mustard, 1 tbsp.
- Cheese, shredded
- Ketchup, ½ cup
- Worcestershire sauce, 1 ½ cup

For Biscuits:

- All-purpose flour, 2 cups
- Shortening, 5 tbsp.
- Baking powder, 2 ½ tsp.
- Milk, ¾ cup
- Salt, ¾ tsp.

ssssssssssssssssssssssssssssssssssssssssssss

Instructions:

Preheat the oven to 400 F.

Combine flour with salt, shortening and baking powder. Pour milk gradually and form smooth dough.

Dust some flour on counter board and roll out the dough into a smooth ball.

Cut into 6 pieces and flatten each piece using a rolling pin and place in a greased muffin tray.

Now cook beef until no longer pink. Add all the remaining ingredients and cook well.

Top each section of the muffin tray with beef mixture and add cheese.

Pop the tray in the oven and bake for 15 minutes or until nicely brown.

7) Shuumai Dumplings

Shuumai skin is square shaped medium sized frozen skin that is easily available at any Japanese store. This shuumai filling can be kept in the freezer for up to a month so you can always make them in bulk and use for up to a month.

Makes: 25 shuumai

Cooking Time: 60 minutes

List of Ingredients:

- Shrimp, 2 pound, coarsely chopped
- Mirin, 1 tbsp.
- Medium onion, ½, chopped
- Soy sauce, 1 tbsp.
- Cornstarch, 1 tbsp.
- Sesame oil, ½ tbsp.
- Ground pork, 4 oz.
- Ginger, 1 tsp., grated
- Ground black pepper, to taste
- Salt, to taste
- Shuumari skin

sssssssssssssssssssssssssssssssssssssssssssss

Instructions:

Mix pork with soy sauce, ginger, mirin and cornstarch and form a smooth paste.

Now add shrimps and onions and combine well. Season with salt and pepper.

Take each shuumai skin and fill the center with the prepared filling.

Enclose the ends together tightly so that the filling won't fall out.

Grease a bowl of steamer slightly and steam the shuumai dumplings for around 15 minutes.

8) Lemony Basil Orzo Pasta Salad

This recipe is a perfect summer treat and includes all the exotic flavors of summer. For more texture, add a can of feta cheese, mushrooms and grilled chicken cubes. This salad is supposed to be served cold so you can conveniently make some extra for next day's lunch.

Makes: 10

Cooking Time: 9 minutes

List of Ingredients:

- Orzo pasta, 1 pound
- Roasted red peppers, ½ cup, chopped
- Lemon zest from 2 large lemons
- Fresh basil, 1 package, chopped
- Olive oil, ½ cup
- Salt, ¼ cup
- Fresh flat leaf parsley, ½ cup, chopped
- Yellow and red grape tomatoes, 2 cups, halved
- Green onions, ½ cup, cut only green part
- Lemon juice, ½ cup

sssssssssssssssssssssssssssssssssssssssssssssss

Instructions:

Cook pasta in salted boiling water for 9 minutes. Drain and set aside DO NOT rinse.

While the pasta is cooking prepare the dressing by combine lemon juice, zest and olive oil together.

Put hot pasta in the dressing and add veggies. Toss well.

Refrigerate overnight or at least 2 hours.

9) Earl Grey Tea Muffins

These easy to cook muffins are way better than succumbing to a greasy doughnut or churros at lunch time. You can also prepare these muffins a night before and just freeze them wrapped in a plastic bag as soon as they become cool enough to handle.

Makes: 10

Cooking Time: 30 minutes

List of Ingredients:

- All-purpose flour, 2 cups minus 3 tbsp.
- Salt, a pinch
- Baking powder, 1 ½ tsp.
- Sucanat or raw cane sugar, 4 tbsp.
- Buttermilk, 1 1/3 cups
- Large eggs, 2
- Earl grey tea leaves, 1 teabag
- Canola oil, 3 tbsp.

sssssssssssssssssssssssssssssssssssssssssssss

Instructions:

Preheat the oven to 360 F.

Grease the muffin tins and keep aside.

Combine all the dry food items together.

Combine all the wet food items together.

Gradually combine the dry ingredients with the wet ingredients and fold well. Do not mix excessively.

Add tea leaves and fold just once.

Fill the muffin tins with the batter and bake for about 20 minutes or until the muffins are puffed and brown.

10) Black Forest Ham and Caramelized Onion Grilled Cheese

The secret ingredient of this recipe is cambozola cheese which is a German blue cheese and is easily available in stores. The texture of this cheese is creamy and compliments rye bread and black forest ham.

Makes: 1

Cooking Time: 10 minutes

List of Ingredients:

- Black forest ham, 2 oz. thinly sliced
- Unsalted butter, 1 tbsp., softened
- Cambozola cheese, 2 oz. thinly sliced
- Caramelized onions, 2 tbsp.
- Light rye bread, 2 slices

sssssssssssssssssssssssssssssssssssssssssssss

Instructions:

Spread butter on each slice and keep aside.

Heat oil in a pan and place buttered slices in the pan with buttered side facing down. Place cheese slices, onion and ham and top it with another buttered slice.

Toast each side for 5 minutes at least.

11) Tamagoyaki

If you don't like the taste of sweetened egg then exclude the sugar completely. To jazz up these tamagoyaki piece, add a slice of bacon over nori sheet and top it with green onions, cheese and wrap and roll in the directed way.

Makes: 3 tamagoyaki

Cooking Time: 3 minutes

List of Ingredients:

- large egg, 1
- Nori sheet, ¼ piece
- Sugar, 1 tsp.

sssssssssssssssssssssssssssssssssssssssssssssss

Instructions:

Beat eggs and sugar together until fluffy.

Grease a nonstick pan with cook spray and pour the egg mixture in the pan.

Keep the heat low as you don't have to cook the egg immediately.

When the egg is half way cooked place nori sheet in the center.

Carefully fold each end of the egg together then roll the crepe vertically and form a tamagoyaki shape.

Cook for 2 minutes and transfer on a paper towel.

Slice into 3 pieces.

12) Sweet Hot Mustard and Jarlsberg Grilled Cheese

Sweet hot mustard pairs greatly with cheese and pretzel rolls. It is a quick snack and keeps you full for a long time. Jarlsberg cheese is easily available at the store. If you don't have soft pretzel rolls, then you can use Dutch crunch roll as a substitute.

Makes: 1

Cooking Time: 15 minutes

List of Ingredients:

- Sweet hot mustard, 2 tsp.
- Soft pretzel roll, 1
- Jarlsberg cheese, 1/3 cup, shredded
- Unsalted butter, 1 tsp., softened

sssssssssssssssssssssssssssssssssssssssssssss

Instructions:

Slice the pretzel roll in half horizontally and flatten it a little with your hands or a rolling pin.

Spread mustard paste in the inner sides of the roll and butter on the outer side.

Heat a nonstick pan and place the roll with buttered side facing the bottom. Add cheese and top it with the remaining half.

Toast each side for 5 minutes.

13) Apple Bunny

These are tiny bunny ears like apples which will make your bento box colorful. These shaped apples are especially made for a kid's bento box. You can cut the wedges in any size depending on the size your box.

Makes: 8 bunnies

Cooking Time: 5 minutes

List of Ingredients:

- Apple, 1
- Water, 2 cups
- Salt, ½ tsp.

sssssssssssssssssssssssssssssssssssssssssssssss

Instructions:

Cut an apple into and then further into eight wedges. Discard the core.

Using a sharp knife mark a V shape on the apple skin and peel off the skin from that area and the excess apple.

Now add apple bunnies in the salted water until you are done preparing all the apples.

Pack in the bento box.

14) Chicken Taco

These chicken tacos are served with healthy corn tortillas. You can pack these tacos with diced tomatoes, pickled cucumbers and salsa on the side. You can also add cheese and sour cream for more flavor.

Makes: 1

Cooking Time: 5 minutes

List of Ingredients:

- Chicken breast, 2, shredded
- Cumin powder, 1 tsp.
- Taco powder, ½ tsp.
- Salt, to taste
- Pepper, to taste
- Corn tortilla, 1

sssssssssssssssssssssssssssssssssssssssssssss

Instructions:

Season shredded chicken with taco powder, salt and cumin.

Fill the corn tortillas with the chicken mixture and enjoy.

15) Sautéed Spinach

Sautéed spinach with corn and seasoned with salt and pepper is an easy to make side dish. It can be paired with mushroom rice and mini meatloaves. You add any kind of veggies in this recipe for example, carrots, cabbage and green peas.

Makes: 1

Cooking Time: 5 minutes

List of Ingredients:

- Frozen spinach
- Ground black pepper, to taste
- Butter, 1 tbsp.
- Frozen corn
- Sea salt, to taste

sssssssssssssssssssssssssssssssssssssssssssss

Instructions:

Melt butter on a nonstick pan.

Add corn and spinach and sauté until spinach wilts.

Allow to cool before packing in the bento box.

16) Mediterranean Tuna Salad

It is a light and healthy salad recipe perfect for your bento lunch box. You can pair this crunchy tuna salad with green grapes, carrots and salsa. This recipe is enough to serve 4 people, which means it will make 4 bento lunch boxes.

Makes: 4

Cooking Time: 20 minutes

List of Ingredients:

- Dijon mustard, 2 tsp.
- Grape tomatoes, 1 pint, halved
- Fresh dill, ¼ cup, chopped
- Kirby cucumber, 1, seeded and chopped
- Pita bread, 2 pieces
- Salt, to taste
- Pepper, to taste
- Scallions, 1 bunch, sliced
- Chickpeas, 1 can of 14 oz. drained and rinsed
- Romaine lettuce, 1 head, shredded
- Extra-virgin olive oil, 1/3 cup
- Solid white tuna in water, 1 can, 12 oz. drained and flaked
- Zest of 1 lemon
- Lemon juice of 1 lemon

sssssssssssssssssssssssssssssssssssssssssssssss

Instructions:

Prepare the dressing by combining lemon juice with mustard and zest. Gradually drizzle olive oil and mix well.

Add dill and season with salt and pepper.

In another bowl combine chickpeas with cucumber, tuna, scallions and tomatoes. Add ¼ cup of the dress and toss well to combine.

Heat a grill pan and brush each side of pita bread with oil. Sprinkle a little pepper and salt.

Grill until for about 2 minutes and slice into wedges.

Combine the remaining dressing with lettuce and add tuna salad.

Pack in the bento box with grilled pita slices.

17) Basic Taco Meat Mix

This recipe makes a long lasting taco filling that you can freeze for up to a month. If you like your tacos extra hot then increase the amount or red chili powder and pepper. Do check the seasoning at the end of the cooking to fix the spices if needed.

Makes: 8 tacos

Cooking Time: 15 minutes

List of Ingredients:

- Lean ground beef, 2 pound
- Red chili powder, 1 tbsp.
- Ground cumin, 1 tsp.
- Red pepper, 1, chopped
- Garlic, 2 cloves, minced
- Water, 1/3 cup
- Sweet paprika powder, 1 tbsp.
- Yellow pepper, 1, chopped
- Onion, 1 medium, chopped
- Tomato paste, 3 tbsp.
- Carrot, 1 medium, chopped
- Ground black pepper, to taste
- Salt, to taste

sssssssssssssssssssssssssssssssssssssssssssss

Instructions:

Sauté the vegetables until tender and soft. Add beef and cook until no longer pink.

Add tomato paste and water. Combine well.

Make a little space in the same pan and sauté the spices until fragrant. Combine the sautéed spices with the meat and season with pepper and salt.

18) Vegetable Pickle Salad

This vegetable pickle salad will last in your refrigerator for weeks so you can easily make it in a large quantity and pack for lunch every alternative day. Pack these sweet and savory pickled vegetables with some radish pickles, bánh mi baguette and strawberries.

Makes: 2

Cooking Time: 5 minutes

List of Ingredients:

- Cabbage, 2 cups, shredded
- Dried red chili peppers, 3
- Carrot, 1 cup, shredded
- Sugar, 4 tbsp.
- Salt, 1 tsp.
- Rice vinegar, ½ cup
- Cucumber, 1 cup, shredded
- Konbu dashi stock granules, 1 tsp.

ssssssssssssssssssssssssssssssssssssssssssssss

Instructions:

Combine all the vegetables together in a large bowl and season with salt. Massage well until some of the veggies wilts.

Now add all the remaining ingredients and cover the bowl tightly with a lid.

Toss well until the veggies combine in the seasoning.

Refrigerate overnight.

19) Bacon-Wrapped Asparagus

Bacon wrapped asparagus is a side dish for a bento lunch box prepared in less than 10 minutes. The crispy wraps are made with sautéed asparagus and rolled with crispy and crunchy bacon strips.

Makes: 2

Cooking Time: 8 minutes

List of Ingredients:

- Asparagus spear, 1, end trimmed
- Ground black pepper, to taste
- Bacon, 1 slice center cut, sliced in halve

sssssssssssssssssssssssssssssssssssssssssssss

Instructions:

Slice asparagus into 6 equal size pieces.

Blanch the pieces in a medium saucepan until firm but tender.

Drain the liquid and allow the asparagus pieces to cool enough to handle.

Lay flat the bacon slices and put 3 pieces of asparagus on each slice and wrap tightly, use a toothpick to enclose the ends firmly.

Heat oil and cook bacon until golden and crispy. Season with pepper.

20) Rafute Rillettes

This recipe makes delicious and juicy pork belly that is cooked for hours to reach its desired doneness. You can pack it in a bento box as it is or use it as spread on bread. It can be kept in the freezer for weeks.

Makes: 4

Cooking Time: 3 hours

List of Ingredients:

- Pork belly, 2 pound
- Raw cane sugar, ½ to ¾ cup
- Sake, 2 cups
- Dark soy sauce, ½ cup
- Fresh ginger, 1 inch piece, sliced
- Dashi stock, 4 cups

ssssssssssssssssssssssssssssssssssssssssssssss

Instructions:

Fill a large pot with water and add pork belly. Add ½ cup of sake and boil on high heat.

Turn the heat low and simmer for 60 minutes.

Drain the water and reserve parboiled pork belly. Trim of any excess fat.

Now use a fork and shred the meat finely. DO NOT use a food processor for this purpose.

Clean the pot and add back the shredded meat into it.

Add remaining sake, dashi and ginger. Add some more water if desired as you have to cover the meat. Bring the mixture to a boil.

Turn the heat low and add sugar. Simmer for 60 minutes.

Cover the pot with foil and punch a few holes in it.

Add soy sauce and simmer for another 60 minutes.

21) Sweet Stewed White Beans

You can substitute white beans for haricot and navy beans. Honey and sugar gives the beans a perfect glossy and caramel look. It is a light but filling side meal for you bento lunch box and can be paired with veggies and a sandwich.

Makes: 2

Cooking Time: 60 minutes

List of Ingredients:

- Dry white beans, 2 cups
- Baking soda, ½ tsp.
- Honey, a tsp.
- Raw cane sugar, ¼ cup
- Soy sauce, 1 tbsp.

sssssssssssssssssssssssssssssssssssssssssssssss

Instructions:

Soak bean overnight in water.

Drain the liquid and transfer the beans to a pot filled with clean water.

Boil the beans and drain the cooking liquid while rinsing the beans in running water.

Again fill the pot with clean water and add beans and baking soda. Simmer on low heat for 40 minutes or until the beans are tender but not mushy.

Add sugar and cook for an additional 30 minutes. Add honey and soy sauce. Simmer for last 15 minutes.

22) Sesame Flavored Beef with Carrot Kinpira

These juicy beef strips are flavored with sesame oil, soy sauce and mirin. It is better if you leave them in the marinade overnight and cook them the next morning. This will also save plenty of your preparation time in the morning. Pack you bento lunch box with beef, carrot kinpira and brown rice.

Makes: 2 bento portions

Cooking Time: 20 minutes

List of Ingredients:

For Beef:

- Beef, 200g, thinly cut
- Mirin, 2 tsp.
- Sesame oil, 2 tsp. + 1 tsp.
- Soy sauce, 2 tsp.
- Brown sugar, 1 tsp.

For Carrot Kinpira:

- Carrots, 2
- Sesame seeds, 1 tsp.
- Dark sesame oil, 1 tbsp.
- Soy sauce, 1 tbsp.
- Red pepper flakes, 1/8 tsp.

ssssssssssssssssssssssssssssssssssssssssssssss

Instructions:

Slice beef into thin strips and mix with soy sauce, 2 tsp. sesame oil, brown sugar and mirin. Combine well. Allow the beef to sit in the marinade for 10 minutes.

Heat 1 tsp. of sesame oil in a nonstick pan and cook beef until done and turns brown.

To make carrot kinpira, slice carrots into thin matchsticks.

Heat sesame oil in a pan and cook carrots for around 5 minutes. Season with red pepper flakes. Add soy sauce and sesame seeds and toss well to combine.

23) Walnut Miso Paste for Cooked Vegetables

Walnut miso paste is ideally used with boiled, blanched and steamed vegetables. It is an easy to make staple and is quite useful as vegetables are an essential part of a bento lunch box. With this miso paste you can add more flavor to the veggies.

Makes: 1/3 cup

Cooking Time: 10 minutes

List of Ingredients:

- Shelled walnut kernels, ½ cup
- Mirin, 1 tbsp.
- Miso, 1 tbsp.
- Raw cane sugar, ½ tbsp.

sssssssssssssssssssssssssssssssssssssssssssssss

Instructions:

Heat a pan and dry-roast the walnuts. Until fragrant and brown. Transfer to a paper towel and let them cool slightly. Now wrap them in the paper towel and rub vigorously so that the outer skin comes off.

Transfer the walnut to a pestle and crush them finely according to your preference.

Mix the crushed walnuts with sugar, mirin and miso. Combine well and store in an air tight container.

24) Vegetable Frittata

This recipe makes a creamy and fluffy vegetable frittata. If you don't have a rice cooker then you can also make it on the stove. To cook your veggies really fast, slice them small and thin, making sure you do not overcook them.

Makes: 2

Cooking Time: 10 minutes

List of Ingredients:

- Small potato, 1, peeled and finely julienned
- Olive oil, 1 tbsp.
- Yellow or red pepper, 1 small, diced
- Small zucchini, 1, cut into thin rounds
- Garlic, 1 whole clove, peeled
- Salt, to taste
- Pepper, to taste

<u>For Egg Mixture:</u>

- Large eggs, 6
- Cheese, 2 tbsp.. Grated
- Olive oil, 1 tbsp.
- Salt, to taste
- Pepper, to taste

sssssssssssssssssssssssssssssssssssssssssssss

Instructions:

Heat 1 tbsp. of oil and garlic clove in a nonstick pan. When the oil had heated up and clove turns brown, discard the clove.

Add veggies and season with pepper and salt. Stir fry until crisp then keep aside.

Drizzle 1 tbsp. of oil in a rice cooker bowl and spread it slightly on the edges.

Add eggs and cheese. Season with pepper and salt. Whisk until foamy.

Spread the veggies in the mixture and place the bowl in the cooker and cook on the regular settings.

25) Mini Cabbage Rolls

These mini cabbage rolls can also be cooked on a stove, you just have to double the cooking time. As this recipe makes quite a lot for 1 or 2 bento lunch boxes, you can freeze the remaining with some of their liquid for up to a month.

Makes: 1 dozen small rolls

Cooking Time: 30 minutes

List of Ingredients:

- Napa cabbage leaves, 12 about 10 inches in size.
- Small onion, 4 tbsp.
- Panko breadcrumbs, 3 tbsp.
- Mixture of ground beef and pork, 12 oz.
- Soy sauce, ½ tbsp.
- Dashi, 3 cups
- Salt, ½ tsp.
- Pepper, to taste
- Fresh ginger, 1 tsp., grated

ssssssssssssssssssssssssssssssssssssssssssssss

Instructions:

Put cabbage leaves in boiling water and boil for 10 minutes.

When the water cools down separate the limp leaves and microwave the remaining and add them back with limp leaves.

Squeeze excess water from the leaves.

Trim out the stems off the leaves in a way that you get a V shape at the end.

Repeat with the remaining leaves.

Now finely chop the stems and mix them with the remaining ingredients in a large bowl. Do not add the leaves.

Take spoonful of the mixture and form 12 balls by rolling the mixture between your palms.

Place the meatballs on the end of each leaf and wrap the sides to enclose the ball completely with the leaf.

Fill the bowl of a rice cooker with dashi and add the leaf balls. Cover the lid and cook on regular settings for 20 minutes.

Strain the liquid and allow to cool down before packing in the bento box.

26) Mushroom Rice and Lemon Chicken Nugget Bento

This recipe makes juicy and flavorful lemon chicken nuggets served with mushroom rice. To add more flavor to the nuggets you can add mirin, masala wine or sake but then reduce the amount of lemon juice by half.

Makes: 2 large bento boxes

Cooking Time: 30 minutes

List of Ingredients:

For Lemon Chicken Nuggets:

- Lemon juice from1 lemon
- Chicken breasts, boneless, skinless and cubed
- Soy sauce, 2 tsp.
- Salt, to taste
- Pepper, to taste
- Olive oil, 1-2 tbsp.
- Cornstarch

For Mushroom Rice:

- Large dried shiitake mushrooms, 2
- Soy sauce, 2 tbsp.
- Kombu seaweed, 1 piece
- Fresh ginger, 1 piece, chopped
- Sake, 1 tbsp.
- White japonica rice, 2 cups
- Mixed mushroom, 1 cup, sliced

sssssssssssssssssssssssssssssssssssssssssss

Instructions:

To prepare nuggets, season with lemon juice from half lemon, salt and pepper. Set aside for 15 minutes.

Heat oil in a nonstick pan.

Evenly coat each chicken cubes in cornstarch and cook until crispy and golden from both side.

Add soy sauce and remaining lemon juice and cook for 5 minutes.

To prepare rice, soak shiitake mushrooms with seaweed in a large bowl filled with water.

Remove mushrooms from the water using a slotted spoon and squeeze any excess water.

Slice it finely and combine with mixed mushrooms and ginger. Season with sake and soy sauce. Keep aside and prepare rice.

Rinse and drain rice at least three times until the water runs clear.

Put them in the rice cooker and add mushrooms along with its liquid. The liquid should be around 2 cups.

Keep rice soaked with mushroom for 60 minutes.

Cook rice accordingly to the normal cooker settings.

27) Mini-Meatloaves

Mini meatloaves can be packed in a bento lunch box with stir fried asparagus seasoned with salt and pepper, along with some sautéed green beans, broccoli, mashed potatoes and tomato slices. They are a true delight!

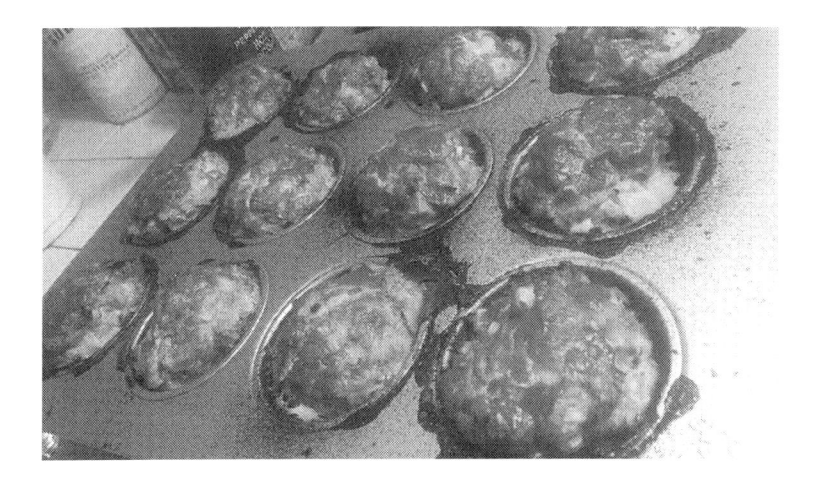

Makes: 10 mini meat loaves

Cooking Time: 15 minutes

List of Ingredients:

- Combination of ground beef, pork and veal, 3 ¼ pound
- Carrot, 1 medium, chopped
- Egg, 1, beaten
- Ground nutmeg, 1 tsp.
- Onion, 2, chopped
- Ground pepper, to taste
- Salt, to taste
- Large sweet bell peppers, 2, chopped
- Breadcrumbs, 1 cup
- Celery stalk of 8 inch in length

sssssssssssssssssssssssssssssssssssssssssssssss

Instructions:

Preheat the oven to 400 F.

Prepare a baking sheet with parchment paper.

Combine all the veggies with beaten egg. Add breadcrumbs and season with nutmeg and pepper.

Gradually combine the beef mixture with the veggies mixture using your hands.

Make 10 equal portions of this mixture and roll between your palms to shape it like a mini loaf.

Assemble them on the prepared baking sheet and pop it in the oven.

Bake for 10 minutes then set the temperature to 330 F and bake for another 30 minutes.

28) Panfried Komachibu

Komachibu are panfried in the soaking liquid of the mushrooms for this recipe. You can use mushrooms later in any other recipe, but until then refrigerate it in its soaking liquid. These crispy komachibu makes a perfect side dish in your bento lunch box. Pair them with fresh fruits and veggies.

Makes: 4

Cooking Time: 10 minutes

List of Ingredients:

- Komachibu/Chikuwabu, 20
- Sugar, ½ tsp.
- Mirin, 1 tbsp.
- Soy sauce, 1 tsp.
- Dried shiitake mushrooms, 3
- Oyster sauce, 1 tbsp.

ssssssssssssssssssssssssssssssssssssssssssssss

Instructions:

Soak mushroom in 2 cups of water overnight.

Soak komachibu for 5 minutes in cold water. Drain and squeeze any excess liquid. Keep aside.

Fill a nonstick pan with 1 cup of mushroom water. Refrigerate the mushroom in the remaining liquid for later use.

Add komachibu in the mushroom liquid and season with soy sauce, oyster sauce, sugar and mirin.

Simmer on low until the liquid has evaporated. Turn the komachibu ¾ times to allow each side to cook well.

29) Poppy Seed Encrusted Green Pea Mini-Burgers

These green colored mini-burgers looks so tempting and are a healthy substitute for fatty burgers. As this recipe makes 10 burgers, you can freeze the remaining cooked burgers for up to 2 weeks.

Cooking Time: 20 minutes

List of Ingredients:

- Frozen peas, 2 cups
- Fresh rosemary, 1 tsp., chopped
- Rice flour, 1 tbsp.
- Tahini, 1 tbsp.
- Black olive paste, 1 tsp.
- Salt, to taste
- Pepper, to taste

<u>For Coating:</u>

- Dried garlic flakes, 1 tsp.
- Black poppy seeds, 3 tbsp.
- Dried onion flakes, 2 tsp.
- Oil, for cooking
- Serving: 10 mini burgers

sssssssssssssssssssssssssssssssssssssssssssss

Instructions:

Add peas with little water in a small pot and season with salt. Bring to a boil on high heat.

Cover the lid and turn the heat low and simmer until peas are cooked well.

Drain the liquid and process the peas along with all the ingredients.

Combine the coating ingredients together in a large plate.

Take spoonful of pea mixture and flatten it to form a mini patty.

Now coat them evenly in the flakes and poppy seeds mixture.

Work in batches and cook each side of the patty for 5 minutes. Do not burn the patties just maintain the crispy texture.

Allow the burgers to cool a little before packing.

30) Pan-fried Crispy Chicken Nuggets with Gobo

You can substitute chicken for turkey in this recipe. Also if you don't have gobo at hand you can use parsnip, carrot or salsify but make sure you have finely julienned them. If you are intending to prepare these nuggets in the morning then simple massage the marinade with your hands and cook the chicken straightway.

Makes: 12 nuggets

Cooking Time: 10 minutes

List of Ingredients:

- Dark meat of chicken, 225g, cut into 12 strips, cooked
- Cornstarch, ½ cup
- Gobo, ¾ cup, finely julienned
- Sake, 1 tbsp.
- Dark soy sauce, 1 tbsp.
- Ginger, 1 tsp., grated
- Vegetable oil, for cooking

sssssssssssssssssssssssssssssssssssssssssssss

Instructions:

Marinate chicken strips with soy sauce, sake and ginger. Refrigerate for ½ hour.

Now add cornstarch and gobo with the chicken and combine well with your hands.

Heat vegetable oil in a pan for deep frying.

Add the mixture and cook until crisp and golden brown on each side.

Transfer the fried chicken on paper towel to drain excess oil.

Allow it to cool a little before packing in the bento box.

About the Author

Allie Allen developed her passion for the culinary arts at the tender age of five when she would help her mother cook for their large family of 8. Even back then, her family knew this would be more than a hobby for the young Allie and when she graduated from high school, she applied to cooking school in London. It had always been a dream of the young chef to study with some of Europe's best and she made it happen by attending the Chef Academy of London.

After graduation, Allie decided to bring her skills back to North America and open up her own restaurant. After 10 successful years as head chef and owner, she decided to sell her business and pursue other career avenues. This monumental decision led Allie to her true calling, teaching. She also started to write e-books for her students to study at home for practice. She is now the proud author of several e-books and gives private and semi-private cooking lessons to a range of students at all levels of experience.

Stay tuned for more from this dynamic chef and teacher when she releases more informative e-books on cooking and baking in the near future. Her work is infused with stores and anecdotes you will love!

Author's Afterthoughts

I can't tell you how grateful I am that you decided to read my book. My most heartfelt thanks that you took time out of your life to choose my work and I hope you find benefit within these pages.

There are so many books available today that offer similar content so that makes it even more humbling that you decided to buying mine.

Tell me what you thought! I am eager to hear your opinion and ideas on what you read as are others who are looking for a good book to buy. Leave a review on Amazon.com so others can benefit from your wisdom!

With much thanks,

Allie Allen

Printed in Great Britain
by Amazon